HARD HAT AND HUSTLE

Pramod Singh Rautela

TANEESHA PUBLISHERS

ISBN : 9789349789968
Edition : First, September 2025
Title : Hard Hat and Hustle
Author : Pramod Singh Rautela

Published by

TANEESHA PUBLISHERS

Regd. Add.: 254, Khuriyakhatta No. 10, Bindukhatta,
Lalkuan, Nainital - 262402, Uttarakhand, India
Website : www.taneeshapublishers.in
E-mail : taneeshapublishers@gmail.com
Phone : +91 8454 812712, +91 8057 812712

Printed by :
Manipal Technologies Limited, Bengaluru - 560001, Karnataka

CONTENTS

Seven Years Inside

CONTENTS

PREFACE

Fresh Graduate —— Associate Manager

I had no clue what I was getting into.

When I walked through those factory gates seven years ago, clutching my engineering degree like it was some kind of shield, I thought I knew what manufacturing was about. Machines, processes, maybe some problem-solving. How hard could it be?

Turns out, everything I thought I knew was wrong.

College taught me equations and theories. The factory floor taught me that people are more complicated than any machine, that pressure can make or break you, and that some of the smartest solutions come from operators who never set foot in a classroom.
I've worked night shifts that felt like they'd never end. I've managed
people twice my age who had every right to doubt me. I've solved problems worth millions of rupees and made mistakes that kept me awake at night. I've been promoted, challenged, frustrated, and proud — sometimes all in the same week.

This isn't another "how to succeed in your career" book. There are plenty of those already, and most of them are written by people who've never had grease under their fingernails or dealt with a production line shutdown at 2 AM.
This is just my story. Seven years of figuring it out as I went along. The good days, the terrible days, and everything in between.

I wrote this for three reasons:
First, for anyone thinking about manufacturing as a career. The reality is messier and harder than the recruitment brochures suggest, but it's also more rewarding than most people realize.
Second, for people already working in manufacturing who sometimes wonder if they made the right choice. You did. What we do matters more than most people understand.
Third, for everyone else who's curious about what actually happens inside those big industrial buildings you see on the highways. It's not what you think.

Manufacturing changed me. It forced me to grow up fast, taught me things about leadership and problem-solving that no classroom could, and showed me that there's real satisfaction in making things that matter.

Would I choose this path again, knowing what I know now?

Absolutely.

But I wish someone had written a book like this before I started. Maybe it would have made those first few years a little less terrifying.

CHAPTER I

FIRST STEPS INTO THE REAL WORLD

The day I got my offer letter from one of India's biggest automotive manufacturers, I felt like I'd won the lottery. After engineering college, countless applications, and nerve-wracking interviews, I was finally going to be a "real" engineer. I had this picture in my head of what it would be like. I'd walk into a clean, modern facility, sit at a computer, design cool stuff, maybe lead some important projects. You know, engineer things. Reality check number one came during the company bus ride on my first day. The bus picked me up at 5 AM. Five in the morning. I'd never been awake at 5 AM voluntarily in my entire life. But there I was, stumbling onto a bus full of people who looked way too alert for that hour. The ride took about an hour through increasingly industrial areas. The buildings got bigger, dirtier, more functional. By the time we reached the plant, we were definitely not in the tech park anymore. The factory was massive. Like, seriously massive. It stretched as far as I could see, with multiple buildings, parking lots full of trucks. The sound hit you first — a constant humming, clanking, mechanical symphony that never stopped.

Week One: Information Overload

My first week was pure orientation. They walked us through every department, explained every process, showed us how raw materials became finished products. It was fascinating and overwhelming at the same time. I remember standing in the welding section, watching sparks fly as robots and humans worked side by side to piece together car frames. The noise was incredible. Even with ear plugs, you had to shout to be heard. Then we visited quality control, where people with microscopes and measuring instruments checked every tiny detail. One small defect could mean scrapping an entire batch. The precision was mindblowing. The maintenance department looked like something out of a movie — massive machines being torn apart and rebuilt, technicians covered in grease solving complex mechanical puzzles. But what struck me most wasn't the technology or the scale. It was the people. Everyone moved with purpose. They knew exactly what they were doing and why it mattered. When a machine made an unusual sound, operators didn't ignore it — they investigated immediately. When a quality issue popped up, teams swarmed to fix it. These weren't just "factory workers" like I'd imagined. These were specialists, problem-solvers, craftspeople who took pride in their work.

CHAPTER I

MEETING MY MANAGER

AT THE END OF MY FIRST WEEK, I WAS ASSIGNED TO RAJESH SIR, A MANAGER WHO'D BEEN WITH THE COMPANY FOR FIFTEEN YEARS. HE WAS THE KIND OF GUY WHO COULD SPOT A PROBLEM FROM ACROSS THE SHOP FLOOR JUST BY THE WAY A MACHINE SOUNDED. "SO," HE SAID DURING OUR FIRST ONE-ON-ONE, "WHAT DO YOU WANT TO DO HERE?" I GAVE HIM SOME TEXTBOOK ANSWER ABOUT PROCESS IMPROVEMENT AND TECHNICAL CHALLENGES. HE SMILED. "THAT'S NICE. BUT FIRST, YOU NEED TO UNDERSTAND HOW THINGS ACTUALLY WORK. YOU'RE GOING TO SPEND TIME IN PRODUCTION. LEARN THE BASICS. THEN WE'LL SEE ABOUT THOSE TECHNICAL CHALLENGES." I WASN'T THRILLED. I WANTED TO JUMP STRAIGHT INTO ENGINEERING WORK, NOT STAND AROUND WATCHING PRODUCTION LINES. BUT RAJESH SIR HAD THIS WAY OF EXPLAINING THINGS THAT MADE YOU REALIZE HOW MUCH YOU DIDN'T KNOW. "SEE, THE THING ABOUT MANUFACTURING," HE SAID, "IS THAT EVERYTHING'S CONNECTED. YOU CAN'T IMPROVE A PROCESS IF YOU DON'T UNDERSTAND WHAT HAPPENS BEFORE AND AFTER IT. YOU CAN'T LEAD PEOPLE IF YOU DON'T KNOW WHAT THEIR JOB IS ACTUALLY LIKE. AND YOU DEFINITELY CAN'T SOLVE PROBLEMS FROM BEHIND A DESK." HE WAS RIGHT, OF COURSE. BUT I DIDN'T REALIZE THAT YET.

THE REAL EDUCATION BEGINS

My second week, they put me on the shop floor with a production team. My job was simple: observe, ask questions, and try not to get in the way. The team leader was Suresh, a guy who'd been running his section for eight years. He knew every machine, every operator, every potential problem. He could predict when a tool needed changing just by listening to the sound it made. "College boy, right?" he said when we first met. Not mean, just matter-of-fact. "Yeah, just graduated." "What did they teach you about production planning?" I launched into some explanation about optimization algorithms and statistical process control. He nodded politely, then pointed to a chart on the wall. "See this? This is what actually matters. How many parts we made yesterday, how many we need to make today, what problems we're dealing with, and who's available to fix them." It was a simple whiteboard with numbers and notes. Nothing fancy. But it told the story of everything happening in that section. Over the next few days, Suresh taught me more about manufacturing than any textbook ever had. How to spot quality issues by eye. Why certain machines needed more attention than others. How small delays could cascade into big problems. How to keep a team motivated during a difficult shift. Most importantly, he taught me that manufacturing isn't just about machines and processes. It's about people making hundreds of small decisions every day that either keep things running smoothly or cause chaos.

CHAPTER I

MY FIRST PROBLEM

Three weeks in, I witnessed my first real crisis. It was a Tuesday afternoon, everything running normally, when suddenly one of the key machines just stopped. Complete shutdown. The whole production line backed up within minutes. I watched as chaos erupted around me. Maintenance technicians appeared from nowhere, managers gathered around the machine, operators from other sections came to help. Everyone knew their role without being told. Rajesh sir was in the middle of it, coordinating the response. He wasn't panicking, wasn't shouting orders. Just calmly organizing people and resources to solve the problem. "What can I do?" I asked him. "Watch and learn," he said. "This is what manufacturing really looks like." For the next two hours, I saw problem-solving in action. They systematically diagnosed the issue, identified the failed component, figured out if they had a replacement, and worked out how to minimize the production impact. It wasn't glamorous. People got dirty, frustrated, tired. But they didn't give up. Step by step, they got the machine running again. When it was over, instead of celebrating, they sat down for what they called a "root cause analysis." They wanted to understand not just what broke, but why it broke, and how to prevent it from happening again. "This is the real job," Rajesh sir told me later. "Not the day-to-day routine, but how you handle the unexpected. That's where you prove yourself."

REALITY SINKS IN

By the end of my first month, a few things had become clear. First, I knew basicall nothing about how manufacturing actually worked. College had taught me theory, bu theory only gets you so far when you're dealing with real machines and real people an real deadlines. Second, this job was going to be way more demanding than I' expected. The hours were long, the pressure was constant, and there was alway something that needed fixing. Third, the people here weren't impressed by m engineering degree. They cared about whether I could contribute, solve problems, an handle responsibility. But fourth, and most importantly, I was starting to realize thi might be exactly what I needed. Every day was different. Every problem was a puzzle t solve. Every small improvement made a real difference. I wasn't sitting in a cubicl writing reports no one would read. I was part of something tangible, something tha mattered. The work was hard, but it was real. And slowly, I was starting to understan what Rajesh sir meant about everything being connected. Manufacturing wasn't jus about making things. It was about solving problems, leading people, and constantl learning. It was about being part of a team that made the impossible happen ever single day. I still had a lot to learn. But for the first time since graduation, I felt like was exactly where I was supposed to be.

CHAPTER II

LIFE ON THE SHOP FLOOR

If you've never worked a manufacturing shift, let me paint you a picture of what a typical day actually looks like. Your alarm goes off at 4:30 AM. Not 4:45, not 5:00. 4:30 sharp. Because the company bus leaves at exactly 5:00, and if you miss it, you're screwed. There's no "running a little late" in manufacturing. The machines don't wait for you. You grab whatever breakfast you can manage at that hour — usually just tea and biscuits — and stumble out to wait for the bus. The streets are empty except for other shift workers heading to various factories around the industrial area. The bus ride is quiet. Everyone's either sleeping or staring out the window, trying to wake up. By the time you reach the plant, though, the energy changes. People start talking, checking their phones for messages from the night shift, mentally preparing for whatever the day might throw at them

THE RHYTHM OF THE FLOOR

By 6 AM, you're on the shop floor, and the place is already humming with activity. The night shift is finishing up, handing over any issues or concerns. Day shift workers are checking equipment, reviewing production targets, getting updated on overnight problems. There's a morning meeting — quick, focused, no nonsense. Production targets for the day. Any quality issues from yesterday. Safety reminders. Equipment status updates. Machine maintenance schedules. It takes maybe ten minutes, but everyone leaves knowing exactly what needs to happen. Then the real work begins. For the next eight to ten hours, you're constantly moving. Checking production numbers. Investigating quality issues. Coordinating with other departments. Troubleshooting equipment problems. Managing people. Putting out fires. The noise level on the shop floor is something you have to experience to understand. It's not just loud — it's a complex symphony of different sounds that tell you what's happening. The steady hum of machines running normally. The sharp crack of metal being cut. The rhythmic thump of stamping presses. The hiss of pneumatic systems. After a while, you learn to read these sounds like a language. When something sounds off, you investigate immediately. Because in manufacturing, small problems become big problems very quickly

CHAPTER II

THE HEAT AND THE HUSTLE

Indian factories in summer are brutal. The heat builds up throughout the day, and by afternoon, it's like working in an oven. You drink water constantly, but you're still dehydrated. Your clothes stick to you. Everyone moves a little slower. But the work doesn't slow down. Production targets don't change because it's hot. Customer deadlines don't move because you're uncomfortable. You learn to push through, to stay focused even when conditions are far from ideal. The pace is relentless. In most office jobs, you have natural breaks — meetings end, you grab coffee, you chat with colleagues. On the shop floor, the machines never stop. The production line keeps moving. If you need a break, someone has to cover for you. This creates a different kind of teamwork. Everyone knows that their colleagues depend on them. If you slack off, someone else has to pick up the slack. If you spot a problem and don't address it, it becomes everyone else's problem.

LEARNING THE UNWRITTEN RULES

Every factory has its official procedures and policies. But the real education comes from learning the unwritten rules — the things that make the difference between surviving and thriving. Like knowing which machines are temperamental and need extra attention. Which operators have the best instincts for spotting problems early. Which supervisors you can approach directly with issues, and which ones need to be handled more diplomatically. You learn who the real experts are — often people who've been there for decades and know more about the equipment than the engineers who designed it. These are the people who can teach you tricks that aren't in any manual. You figure out the rhythm of the factory. Which times of day are most stressful. When you can grab a few minutes to think about bigger issues. How to time your conversations with busy colleagues. When to push for immediate action versus when to be patient.

THE PEOPLE WHO MAKE IT WORK

What surprised me most about factory work was how much it depends on relationships. You might think it's all about machines and processes, but really, it's about people. There's the operator who notices when a machine sounds slightly different and flags it before it becomes a major problem. The maintenance technician who can fix anything but gets frustrated with excessive paperwork. The quality inspector who takes pride in catching defects that others miss. The supervisor who's been there for twenty years and can predict production issues before they happen. The material handler who knows exactly where to find any component in the warehouse. The shift leader who can keep everyone motivated during tough periods. Each person has their own personality, their own way of working, their own pet peeves and strengths. Learning to work effectively with this diverse group of people — many of whom are older and more experienced than you — is one of the biggest challenges of factory work.

WHEN THINGS GO WRONG

In manufacturing, Murphy's Law isn't just a saying — it's a daily reality. Whatever can go wrong will go wrong, usually at the worst possible time. Machines break down during the most critical production runs. Quality issues appear just before customer shipments. Key people call in sick on the busiest days. Supply chain problems create material shortages. Power outages shut down entire sections. What I learned is that how you handle these crises defines you more than anything else. Anyone can manage when things are running smoothly. The real test is what you do when everything's falling apart. I've seen people crack under pressure, making bad decisions that make problems worse. I've also seen people stay calm, methodically work through issues, and somehow pull victory from the jaws of disaster. The veterans taught me that most problems have been solved before. The trick is staying calm enough to think clearly, asking the right people for help, and not making emotional decisions when you're stressed.

THE SATISFACTION OF MAKING THINGS WORK

Despite all the challenges — the early hours, the heat, the pressure, the constant problems — there's something deeply satisfying about manufacturing work. When you solve a complex technical problem that's been plaguing production for weeks, it feels amazing. When you implement an improvement that increases efficiency or quality, you can see the immediate impact. When you help train someone new and watch them develop confidence and skills, it's incredibly rewarding. There's also something primal about making things. At the end of each day, you can point to tangible results of your work. Products that will be used by real people. Problems that are actually solved. Improvements that make a genuine difference. In our hyper-digital world, where so much work feels abstract and disconnected from reality, manufacturing keeps you grounded. The work is real, the challenges are concrete, and the results are measurable.

FINDING YOUR RHYTHM

It took me several months to really find my rhythm on the shop floor. To stop feeling overwhelmed by the constant demands and start feeling capable of handling whatever came up. Part of it was developing physical stamina — getting used to being on my feet all day, working in challenging conditions, maintaining focus for long periods. Part of it was developing mental resilience — learning not to panic when problems arose, building confidence in my ability to figure things out, accepting that some days would just be harder than others. But mostly it was about finding my place within the larger system. Understanding how my role fit into the bigger picture. Building relationships with colleagues. Earning respect through competence and reliability rather than just credentials. Once I found that rhythm, the work became not just manageable but genuinely engaging. Each day brought new challenges, new opportunities to learn, new chances to contribute something meaningful. The shop floor taught me lessons about leadership, problem-solving, and persistence that I never could have learned in a classroom. It showed me what I was capable of when pushed outside my comfort zone. And it gave me a deep appreciation for the people who make manufacturing work — the skilled professionals who show up every day, handle whatever challenges arise, and somehow keep everything running smoothly. These are the people who really make India's economy work. And I was proud to be one of them

"I thought manufacturing was about machines and processes. Turns out, it's about people, pressure, and learning to solve problems that don't exist in textbooks."

CHAPTER III

TAKING CHARGE — MY FIRST BIG WIN

Six months into my job, I was starting to feel like I understood the basics. I could navigate the shop floor without getting lost, I knew most people's names, and I had a decent grasp of our production processes. But I was still essentially following other people's lead, helping with their projects, learning the ropes. That changed when Rajesh sir called me into his office one Tuesday morning. "We have a situation," he said, pulling up some cost projections on his computer. "The company wants to install a new robotic system programme for the assembly line. They've gotten quotes from suppliers — around 15 lakh rupees for the complete setup." I nodded, wondering why he was telling me this. "Here's the thing," he continued. "Before we spend that money, I want to see if we can build something ourselves. Think of it as a proof of concept. If we can make it work in-house, we save a lot of money and learn something in the process." My heart started beating faster. "You want me to try building a robotic system?" "I want you to figure out if it's possible. Look at what we need, what we have available, what it would take to make it work. If you think it's feasible, we'll give you the resources to try." I'd never built a robot in my life. I'd studied robotics in college, sure, but that was all theoretical. This was asking me to create something that would actually be used in production, that would affect real schedules and real costs. "What's the timeline?" I asked. "Two months to show me a working prototype. If it works, we'll implement it. If it doesn't, we go with the supplier quote." I walked out of that meeting terrified and excited in equal measure. This was my chance to prove I could contribute something real, something valuable. But it was also a chance to fail spectacularly in front of everyone.

Research and Planning

The first week was pure research. I studied our existing assembly process, identified exactly what the robot needed to do, and figured out what things we'd need. I spent hours in the technical library, reading about servo motors, sensors, programming languages, control systems. I talked to our maintenance team about what programme we already had. I reached out to suppliers about sharing any existing programming. Slowly, a plan started to emerge. We could use an existing programme with some modifications.

The Build Process

Building the programme was like solving a hundred small puzzles simultaneously. Every component had to work perfectly on its own and integrate seamlessly with everything else. . Our first attempt was too rigid and couldn't handle minor variations in programming . Our second attempt was too flexible and wasn't precise enough. Finally, we found the right balance of strength and adaptability.
. But the programming was where I spent most of my time. Teaching the robot to recognize different axis and move accordingly I worked late most nights, running tests, debugging code, trying different approaches. Sometimes I'd think I had everything working perfectly, only to discover a new edge case that broke the whole system. The team was incredibly patient with my learning process. When I got stuck, they'd offer practical suggestions. When something wasn't working, they'd help me understand why. When I got frustrated, they'd remind me that all complex projects go through difficult phases.

The Impact

Six months later, we calculated the actual savings from the project. Between the reduced component costs, improved production efficiency, and labor reallocation, we'd saved the company over 12 lakh rupees in the first year alone. More importantly for me personally, I'd proven that I could take on significant responsibility and deliver results. I wasn't just the new guy learning the ropes anymore — I was someone who could identify opportunities, lead technical projects, and create real value. The success opened doors for me. Rajesh sir started giving me more complex assignments. Other departments began asking for my input on their technical challenges. I'd learned that I could figure out things I'd never done before, that I could build effective teams around complex projects, that I could handle pressure and deliver results when it mattered

CHAPTER IV

AFTER HOURS — LIFE IN THE INDUSTRIAL ZONE

People always ask me what it's like living near a factory. The short answer? It's not like the movies. Our plant is about 45 minutes outside the main city, in one of those industrial zones that seems to exist in its own world. Rows of factories, warehouses, and manufacturing units stretch as far as you can see. During the day, it's bustling with trucks, workers, and the constant hum of industry. At night, it becomes almost eerily quiet except for the plants that run 24/7. Most of us live nearby rentals. My first place was a basic room in a housing complex about 15 minutes from the plant. Concrete walls, basic furniture, shared common areas. Nothing fancy, but it was clean and convenient. The thing about industrial areas is that they're built for function, not comfort. There aren't many cafes, shopping malls, or entertainment options. What you get instead is a tight-knit community of people who all face similar challenges and understand each other's lives.

THE SOCIAL REALITY

When I tell friends from college where I live and work, I can see them trying not to look sorry for me. They're working in gleaming office buildings in the city, having lunch at fancy restaurants, going to rooftop bars after work. Meanwhile, I'm dealing with dust, noise, and limited transport options. The nearest movie theater is a 30-minute bus ride away. Good restaurants are even scarcer. Weekend entertainment usually means traveling back to the city. But here's what they don't understand: there's something liberating about the simplicity. Without constant distractions, you focus on what actually matters. Work, relationships, personal growth. You're not spending hours in traffic or enormous amounts of money just to maintain a lifestyle. Plus, the people you meet in industrial areas are different. They're practical, hardworking, down-to-earth. They judge you based on what you contribute, not what you wear or where you went to college.

CHAPTER 4

WEEKEND ESCAPES

Weekends become precious in a way they never were during college. Saturday mornings, those of us with energy would catch the early bus into the city. It felt like entering a different world — clean streets, air conditioning, people dressed up for leisure instead of work. We'd walk through malls just to experience the environment. Sit in cafes for hours, savoring the luxury of not having anywhere urgent to be. Watch movies in comfortable theaters. Meet up with friends from other industries and hear about their completely different work experiences. But by Sunday evening, there was always this pull back to the industrial zone. Back to the place where work happened, where real things got made, where you felt like you were part of something important. Some of my colleagues never adjusted to this lifestyle. They lasted six months, maybe a year, before moving to jobs closer to the city center. The isolation, the limited social options, the stark difference from college life — it was too much for them. Others, like me, found a different kind of satisfaction in it. We learned to create our own entertainment, to appreciate simpler pleasures, to find meaning in work itself rather than in the lifestyle it afforded.

BUILDING REAL FRIENDSHIPS

One unexpected benefit of industrial living is the quality of friendships you develop. When you're not constantly rushing between social events and entertainment options, you actually have time to get to know people. My closest friends became the guys I worked with. We'd grab dinner together after tough shifts, help each other move to new apartments, celebrate each other's successes and commiserate over failures. These weren't the casual friendships of college or the networking relationships of corporate life. These were people who understood the reality of your daily existence, who had been through similar challenges, who could offer practical advice and genuine support. We'd organize weekend trips to nearby hill stations, pooling resources to rent a car and split accommodation costs. We'd cook together in shared kitchens, experimenting with different regional cuisines based on where everyone was from. During festivals, those of us who couldn't go home would celebrate together, creating makeshift families away from our real ones.

STAYING CONNECTED

One challenge of industrial life is maintaining relationships with friends who've chosen different career paths. While you're dealing with production crises and equipment failures, they're attending team lunches and office parties. Social media makes this easier and harder at the same time. You can stay connected with everyone's lives, but the differences become more apparent. Your college friends are posting from weekend getaways and work conferences. You're posting... what? Pictures of machines? I learned to appreciate both worlds without feeling inferior about either. My work might not be as Instagram-friendly, but it was real and important. My lifestyle might not be as convenient, but it was authentic and grounding. The key was finding pride in what you were actually doing rather than comparing external circumstances. Manufacturing work gives you skills, experiences, and perspectives that office jobs simply can't. Learning to value those differences instead of feeling defensive about them makes all the difference.

PERSONAL PROJECTS AND HOBBIES

With fewer external distractions, you have more time and mental space for personal interests. Many of my colleagues developed hobbies and side projects that they never would have had time for in busier urban environments. Some learned new technical skills — programming, electronics, mechanical design — that complemented their work but expanded their capabilities. Others pursued completely different interests — music, writing, photography — that provided creative outlets from the technical demands of manufacturing. I started a podcast during this time, interviewing other young engineers about their career journeys and challenges. It became a way to connect with people beyond my immediate circle, to explore different perspectives on manufacturing and engineering careers. The podcast grew slowly but steadily, eventually reaching engineering students and young professionals across India. It became something I was proud of, a contribution to the broader engineering community that was entirely separate from my day job.

THE VALUE OF SIMPLICITY

Looking back on those early years in the industrial zone, I realize how much the lifestyle shaped me. The simplicity forced me to focus on essentials. The limited options made me more resourceful and creative. The tight community taught me the value of genuine relationships. Would I have learned the same lessons living in a fancy apartment in the city center? Probably not. The convenience and constant stimulation of urban life can actually be distracting from personal and professional development. In the industrial zone, success was measured differently. Not by where you lived or what you owned, but by how well you did your job, how you treated your colleagues, how you handled challenges. It taught me that happiness and fulfillment don't require perfect circumstances. They come from finding meaning in your work, building good relationships, and maintaining perspective on what actually matters. The industrial lifestyle isn't for everyone, and that's okay. But for those who can adapt to it, it offers something unique — a chance to focus on substance over style, to develop resilience and resourcefulness, to be part of communities built around shared purpose rather than shared consumption.

CHAPTER V

WHAT THE FACTORY TAUGHT ME (THAT COLLEGE DIDN'T)

Engineering college taught me a lot about theory, equations, and ideal conditions. Six months on the factory floor taught me how little any of that mattered when dealing with real problems, real people, and real constraints. Don't get me wrong — the technical foundation from college was important. Understanding principles of physics, mathematics, and engineering gave me the framework to approach complex problems systematically. But the gap between textbook knowledge and practical application was enormous.

Here are the biggest lessons I learned that no classroom could have taught me

PEOPLE SKILLS MATTER MORE THAN TECHNICAL SKILLS

This was the hardest lesson for me to accept. I'd always been the guy who could solve technical problems, who understood complex concepts, who got the highest grades on exams. I thought that would be enough. Wrong. On the factory floor, technical competence is just the entry fee. What determines your success is how well you work with people — operators, technicians, supervisors, colleagues from other departments. I learned this when I tried to implement a "simple" process improvement early in my career. The math was perfect, the engineering was sound, the benefits were obvious. But I hadn't bothered to really understand how the operators currently did their jobs, what challenges they faced, or why they might be resistant to change. The result? My brilliant improvement sat unused while people found ways to work around it. Ravi, one of the senior operators, finally took me aside. "Your idea isn't bad," he said, "but you never asked us what we thought. You just assumed we'd do whatever you designed." He was right. I'd been so focused on the technical solution that I'd ignored the human element entirely. From that day forward, I made it a point to involve people in problem-solving rather than just presenting them with solutions. The results were dramatically better, and I learned way more in the process.

CHAPTER V

EVERYTHING IS CONNECTED

In college, we studied systems in isolation. Thermodynamics in one class, materials science in another, manufacturing processes in a third. Each subject had clear boundaries and well-defined inputs and outputs. Real manufacturing doesn't work that way. Everything affects everything else. A quality issue in one department creates scheduling problems in another. A maintenance delay affects production targets, which affects customer deliveries, which affects sales commitments, which affects financial performance. A change in raw material specifications requires adjustments in processing parameters, which affects quality control procedures, which requires operator retraining, which impacts productivity until everyone gets up to speed. Learning to think systematically — to consider the broader implications of any decision or change — became crucial for effectiveness. You couldn't optimize one part of the process without understanding how it would affect other parts. This systems thinking became one of my most valuable skills. It helped me identify root causes rather than just symptoms, design solutions that actually worked in practice, and anticipate problems before they became crises

URGENCY IS EVERYTHING

College operates on semester timelines. You have months to complete projects, weeks to study for exams, multiple chances to improve your performance. Manufacturing operates on shift timelines. If a machine breaks down, you have hours or minutes to fix it before it affects production targets. If a quality issue emerges, you need to identify and correct it immediately before it affects customer shipments. This urgency isn't artificial pressure created by demanding managers. It's the reality of serving customers who depend on your products, meeting commitments that affect other people's businesses, and managing costs that determine whether your company remains competitive. Learning to work effectively under pressure, to make good decisions quickly, to prioritize ruthlessly when everything seems important — these skills don't develop in low-stakes academic environments. I remember my first production crisis, when a key machine failed during a critical customer delivery. The pressure was intense, but it taught me that I could think clearly and act decisively even when everything was chaotic. That confidence in handling urgent situations became invaluable throughout my career

CHAPTER V

CONTINUOUS LEARNING IS NON-NEGOTIABLE

In college, learning was episodic. You studied hard before exams, then relaxed until the next assessment period. You learned what was required for specific courses, then moved on to new subjects. In manufacturing, learning never stops. Technology evolves constantly. Customer requirements change. Regulations get updated. New materials and processes become available. Competitors develop better approaches. If you stop learning, you become obsolete very quickly. The operators who've been successful for decades are the ones who continuously adapt to new equipment, new procedures, new challenges. I developed the habit of reading technical journals, attending training sessions, experimenting with new approaches, and seeking advice from colleagues who knew more than I did. This curiosity and continuous learning became more important than any specific knowledge I'd gained in college

LEADERSHIP CAN'T BE TAUGHT FROM BOOKS

College courses on management and leadership are fine for understanding basic concepts, but they don't prepare you for the reality of leading people who are older, more experienced, and sometimes skeptical of your authority. I learned leadership by watching effective leaders in action, making mistakes and learning from them, and gradually earning respect through competence and consistency. The best leaders I worked with didn't rely on their formal authority. They influenced people through expertise, fairness, and genuine concern for their team's success. They made tough decisions when necessary but explained their reasoning. They gave credit generously and took responsibility for failures. Learning to lead people who don't have to follow you — because they could easily find other jobs or request transfers — teaches you to lead through influence rather than authority. This made me a much more effective leader later in my career.

PROBLEM-SOLVING IS AN ART, NOT A SCIENCE

Engineering courses teach systematic approaches to problem-solving: define the problem, gather data, analyze options, implement solutions, measure results. Real-world problem-solving is messier. You often don't have complete information. Time constraints prevent thorough analysis. Multiple problems interact with each other. Solutions that work in theory fail in practice for unexpected reasons. I learned to be comfortable with uncertainty, to make decisions with incomplete information, to iterate quickly rather than seeking perfect solutions. The best problem-solvers I worked with combined analytical thinking with intuition, technical knowledge with practical experience, systematic approaches with creative flexibility

CHAPTER V

QUALITY IS EVERYONE'S RESPONSIBILITY

In college, quality was something you worried about during design and testing phases. In manufacturing, quality is a constant concern for everyone involved in the process. Operators checking dimensions throughout production. Technicians maintaining equipment to prevent defects. Engineers designing processes that are inherently stable. Supervisors catching problems before they become bigger issues. I learned that preventing quality problems is always more effective than fixing them after they occur. This required understanding not just what could go wrong, but why it might go wrong and how to build safeguards into processes. This focus on prevention rather than correction became a core part of how I approach any complex project.

RESILIENCE IS A SKILL YOU DEVELOP

College challenges are temporary and largely predictable. Study hard, complete assignments, pass exams, move to the next level. Manufacturing challenges are ongoing and often unpredictable. Equipment failures, supply chain disruptions, customer changes, regulatory updates, personnel issues — problems arise constantly and require constant adaptation. Building resilience — the ability to handle setbacks, learn from failures, and maintain effectiveness under stress — became essential for long-term success. I learned that resilience isn't a personality trait you either have or don't have. It's a skill you develop through experience, practice, and conscious effort to maintain perspective during difficult periods.

PRACTICAL WISDOM MATTERS MORE THAN THEORETICAL KNOWLEDGE

The most valuable insights often came from people with years of hands-on experience rather than advanced degrees. Operators who could diagnose problems by sound or vibration. Technicians who knew exactly which tools worked best for specific tasks. Supervisors who could predict how different people would react to changes. This practical wisdom — gained through years of daily problem-solving — was often more valuable than theoretical knowledge for getting things done effectively. I learned to seek out and respect this practical expertise, to combine it with my technical background to develop better solutions than either approach could achieve alone.

SUCCESS REQUIRES BOTH INDIVIDUAL EXCELLENCE AND TEAM EFFECTIVENESS

College rewards individual achievement. Your grades depend on your own performance, and collaboration is often considered cheating. Manufacturing success depends on team performance. Individual excellence that doesn't contribute to team effectiveness is useless. Team success that doesn't recognize individual contributions is unsustainable. Learning to balance personal development with team contribution, to compete and collaborate simultaneously, to take responsibility for both individual and collective results — these skills were crucial for advancement and effectiveness.

THE REAL WORLD IS ALWAYS MORE COMPLEX THAN MODELS

Engineering education relies heavily on simplified models that capture essential elements while ignoring complicating factors. These models are useful for understanding principles and solving specific problems. Real manufacturing involves countless variables that don't appear in textbooks. Human behavior, equipment variations, environmental factors, supply chain complexities, regulatory requirements, cost constraints. I learned to use models and analysis as starting points rather than final answers, to always validate theoretical solutions against practical constraints, and to remain humble about the limitations of any analytical approach. These lessons didn't replace my technical education — they built upon it. The combination of solid technical foundations and practical wisdom gained through experience became the basis for everything I accomplished in my manufacturing career. More importantly, these lessons shaped how I approach any complex challenge: with respect for both technical rigor and practical constraints, with emphasis on people and systems rather than just technology, and with the understanding that continuous learning and adaptation are essential for long

CHAPTER VI

WHEN THE PRESSURE GETS REAL

If you think college exams are stressful, try managing a production line that's behind schedule with a customer delivery deadline looming and a key machine that just started making weird noises. Manufacturing pressure isn't like academic pressure. In college, if you mess up an exam, you might get a bad grade or have to retake a course. In manufacturing, if you mess up, it can cost hundreds of thousands of rupees, affect customer relationships, or impact people's jobs. The pressure is constant, relentless, and often unpredictable. And learning to handle it effectively isn't just important for your career — it's essential for your sanity.

THE DAILY DRUMBEAT

Every day starts with numbers. Production targets, quality metrics, efficiency goals, cost objectives. These aren't suggestions or guidelines — they're commitments that determine whether the day is considered successful or not. The targets aren't set arbitrarily. They're based on customer orders, capacity calculations, historical performance, and competitive requirements. Meeting them consistently is what keeps the factory profitable and people employed. But targets are just numbers until you try to achieve them with real equipment, real materials, and real people dealing with real problems. That's where the pressure begins. Equipment breaks down. Raw materials arrive late or don't meet specifications. People call in sick. Quality issues require investigation and correction. Supply chain problems create shortages. Power outages shut down production. Each of these problems threatens your ability to meet targets. Each requires immediate attention and creative problem-solving. Each adds stress to an already demanding environment.

CHAPTER VI

WHEN EVERYTHING GOES WRONG AT ONCE

Murphy's Law isn't just a saying in manufacturing — it's a weekly reality. The worst problems always seem to happen at the worst possible times. I'll never forget the day we had a perfect storm of problems. A key machine broke down just as we were starting our largest production run of the month. The replacement part was stuck in customs. Our backup supplier was out of stock. The customer was demanding confirmation of delivery dates. Meanwhile, a quality issue from the previous day required us to inspect and potentially rework thousands of finished parts. The quality team was stretched thin, production was backing up, and management was asking for hourly updates on both situations. To make things worse, two operators called in sick, leaving us short-staffed during the most challenging shift of the month. By 10 AM, it felt like everything that could go wrong had gone wrong. The stress level in the factory was palpable. People were moving faster, talking more urgently, making more phone calls. But here's what I learned: this is when you find out what you and your team are really made of.

LEARNING TO STAY CALM UNDER FIRE

My natural instinct during crises was to panic, to rush around trying to fix everything at once, to make quick decisions without thinking through consequences. This approach makes everything worse. Suresh, one of the senior supervisors, pulled me aside during that terrible day. "Take a breath," he said. "Panicking doesn't solve problems faster. It just makes you more likely to create new problems." He was right. The most effective people during crises were the ones who stayed calm, thought systematically, and made deliberate decisions even under pressure. I learned to pause, even for just a few seconds, before reacting to urgent problems. To ask myself: What's the real issue here? What are my options? What are the likely consequences of each option? Who can help me solve this? This systematic approach to crisis management became one of my most valuable skills. It helped me make better decisions under pressure and gave confidence to the people around me who were also dealing with stress.

THE WEIGHT OF RESPONSIBILITY

What makes manufacturing pressure different from academic pressure is the scope of responsibility. Your decisions affect not just your own performance, but the performance of entire teams, the success of important projects, and sometimes the financial health of the company. When you're responsible for meeting production targets that affect customer deliveries, the pressure isn't just professional — it's personal. You know that failing to deliver could damage long-term customer relationships, affect your colleagues' bonuses, or even threaten people's job security. This weight of responsibility can be overwhelming if you let it. But it can also be motivating if you channel it properly. I learned to use the pressure as fuel for better performance rather than letting it create paralysis. The knowledge that other people were counting on me made me more focused, more creative, more persistent in finding solutions.

CHAPTER VI

BUILDING PRESSURE TOLERANCE

Like physical fitness, pressure tolerance is something you build gradually through experience and conscious effort. My first few months, every production problem felt like a major crisis. The adrenaline rush was exhausting, and I'd go home mentally drained even when the actual problems were relatively minor. Over time, I developed better perspective on what constituted a real emergency versus a normal challenge. I learned to differentiate between problems that required immediate action and problems that could be addressed more thoughtfully. I also learned practical techniques for managing stress during difficult periods. Taking short breaks to clear my head. Talking through problems with experienced colleagues. Breaking large problems into smaller, manageable tasks. Celebrating small victories even during difficult periods.

THE IMPORTANCE OF SUPPORT SYSTEMS

Nobody handles pressure well in isolation. The people who thrived under manufacturing stress were those who built strong support networks within the factory. Colleagues who could provide technical expertise when you were stuck. Supervisors who could offer perspective based on their experience. Operators who could suggest practical solutions you hadn't considered. These relationships weren't just professional — they were personal. People who understood the unique stresses of manufacturing work, who had been through similar challenges, who could offer both practical advice and emotional support. Building these relationships during normal times made them available during crisis periods. People were more willing to help when they knew you genuinely cared about their success and weren't just using

LEARNING FROM PRESSURE SITUATIONS

Every high-pressure situation taught me something valuable, even when the immediate results weren't perfect. I learned which types of problems I handled well and which required me to seek help quickly. I learned which decision-making approaches worked under pressure and which led to mistakes. I learned how to communicate effectively during crises without creating additional panic or confusion. Most importantly, I learned that pressure situations were opportunities to demonstrate capability and build trust with colleagues and management. People notice how you handle difficult challenges, and proving yourself during tough periods opens doors for future opportunities.

THE SATISFACTION OF COMING THROUGH

While manufacturing pressure can be exhausting and stressful, there's also something deeply satisfying about successfully handling difficult challenges. When you pull together as a team to solve multiple problems simultaneously, when you find creative solutions under tight deadlines, when you deliver results despite seemingly impossible obstacles — the sense of achievement is incredible. These victories create confidence that carries over to future challenges. You know that you can handle whatever comes up because you've already proven it to yourself and others. The pressure also creates strong bonds with colleagues who've been through similar experiences. There's a camaraderie among people who've worked together during difficult periods that's different from normal professional relationship

MAINTAINING PERSPECTIVE

The key to handling manufacturing pressure sustainably is maintaining perspective on both the importance and the limitations of any individual challenge. Yes, meeting production targets matters. Yes, solving problems quickly is important. Yes, customer satisfaction affects everyone's long-term success. But no single problem, no matter how urgent it seems in the moment, is worth sacrificing your health, your relationships, or your long-term effectiveness. I learned to give maximum effort during crises while also maintaining boundaries that allowed me to recover and prepare for future challenges. To care deeply about results while not taking failures personally. To push hard when necessary while also recognizing when problems were beyond my control. This balance — between caring enough to perform well under pressure but not so much that the pressure becomes destructive — took years to develop but became essential for long-term success in manufacturing. The pressure never completely goes away. Even as you advance in your career and gain more experience, new challenges create new types of stress. But learning to handle pressure effectively — to use it as motivation rather than letting it become overwhelming — is one of the most valuable skills you can develop in any demanding career.

CHAPTER VII

PEOPLE ARE COMPLICATED

Technical problems, I could handle. Give me a machine that's not working properly, a process that needs optimization, or a quality issue that requires root cause analysis, and I could figure it out systematically. People problems? That was a whole different level of complexity. My biggest wake-up call came about eight months into my job, when I was put in charge of a small project team that included operators, technicians, and engineers from different departments. On paper, it looked straightforward. We had clear objectives, defined timelines, and all the necessary resources. What could go wrong? Everything, as it turned out. But not for technical reasons.

THE AGE GAP CHALLENGE

The most immediate challenge was that half my team was significantly older than me. Rajesh had been operating machinery since before I was born. Priya had fifteen years of quality control experience. Kumar knew more about electrical systems than most engineers. They were polite during our first team meeting, but I could see the skepticism in their eyes. Who was this kid to tell them how to do their jobs? I made the mistake of trying to establish authority through my title and technical credentials. Big mistake. After a few weeks of minimal progress and obvious resistance, Rajesh finally spoke up. "Sir, with respect, you're trying to manage us like we're machines. But we're people with our own ideas and experiences." He was absolutely right. I'd been so focused on project timelines and technical requirements that I'd ignored the human element entirely.

CHAPTER VII

LEARNING TO LISTEN FIRST

That conversation changed my entire approach to leadership. Instead of starting with what I wanted people to do, I started by understanding what they thought about the challenges we were facing. Rajesh had insights about equipment behavior that weren't in any manual. Priya had seen quality patterns that could help us prevent problems rather than just detect them. Kumar had ideas for improving processes that I never would have considered. When I actually listened to their perspectives, two things happened. First, our solutions became much better because they incorporated practical knowledge I didn't have. Second, people became invested in the project's success because they felt like contributors rather than just order-takers. This lesson — that listening is more important than talking when you're trying to lead people — became fundamental to everything I did afterward.

MANAGING DIFFERENT PERSONALITIES

Every person brought different strengths, motivations, and challenges to the team. Learning to work with these differences rather than fighting them became crucial for project success. Ramesh was incredibly detail-oriented and thorough, but he moved slowly and resisted any changes to established procedures. I learned to give him time to think through new approaches and to use his thoroughness as a quality check on other people's work. Sita was creative and energetic, always suggesting new ideas, but she sometimes jumped to solutions before fully understanding problems. I learned to channel her enthusiasm while asking questions that helped her think through implications. Manoj was quiet and rarely spoke up in group meetings, but his insights were usually the most valuable when he did share them. I learned to create opportunities for him to contribute in smaller settings where he was more comfortable. Managing these different styles required me to adjust my communication approach constantly. What motivated one person discouraged another. What worked for building confidence in one team member created overconfidence in another

THE TRUST FACTOR

The most important lesson was that technical competence alone doesn't create trust. People need to believe that you care about their success, not just the project's success. This meant understanding their career goals, acknowledging their contributions publicly, and protecting them when things went wrong. It meant being honest about challenges and uncertainties rather than pretending I had all the answers. Building this trust took time and consistency. People watched how I handled pressure, how I treated different team members, how I responded when they made mistakes or disagreed with my decisions. The breakthrough came during a particularly difficult phase when equipment problems threatened our timeline. Instead of panicking or blaming people, I focused on problem-solving and kept the team updated on our options and constraints. After we worked through the crisis successfully, the team's attitude toward me changed completely. They started coming to me with ideas and concerns before problems became urgent. They took ownership of solutions rather than just implementing my instructions.

CHAPTER VII

CULTURAL COMPLEXITY

Working in Indian manufacturing means dealing with layers of cultural complexity that textbooks don't prepare you for. Regional differences in communication styles, work habits, and social expectations. Generational differences in attitudes toward authority, change, and professional development. Educational differences that affect how people process information and make decisions. I learned not to assume that everyone shared my background, values, or perspectives. What seemed like obvious common sense to me might be completely foreign to someone with different experiences. This required constant attention to how I communicated, how I structured work, and how I provided feedback. What worked with one person could be completely ineffective with anothe

CONFLICT RESOLUTION

People disagreements were inevitable when you brought together different personalities under pressure to deliver results. Learning to address conflicts constructively rather than ignoring them or making them worse became a critical skill. Most conflicts weren't really about the technical issues that triggered them. They were about respect, recognition, communication breakdowns, or competing priorities. I learned to address conflicts early, before they became personal or affected team performance. To focus on understanding different perspectives rather than determining who was right or wrong. To find solutions that addressed underlying concerns rather than just surface symptoms. The key was creating an environment where people felt safe expressing disagreements and confident that conflicts would be resolved fairly rather than ignored or decided arbitrarily.

THE MOTIVATION QUESTION

Different people were motivated by completely different things. Some cared most about learning new skills. Others wanted recognition for their expertise. Some were focused on career advancement. Others prioritized job security or work-life balance. Understanding these different motivations helped me assign tasks, provide feedback, and create incentives that actually worked for individual team members. For example, giving Rajesh opportunities to mentor newer team members motivated him much more than promises of future promotions. Providing Sita with exposure to different departments satisfied her curiosity and kept her engaged. This personalized approach to motivation required more effort than treating everyone the same, but it was dramatically more effective for team performance and individual satisfaction.

CHAPTER VII

CULTURAL COMPLEXITY

The most successful teams I worked with weren't necessarily the ones with the most talented individuals. They were the ones where people genuinely liked working together and brought out the best in each other. This chemistry didn't happen automatically. It required conscious effort to create opportunities for people to get to know each other beyond their professional roles, to find common ground, and to develop mutual respect. Simple things like taking time for informal conversations, celebrating successes together, and supporting each other during difficult periods made enormous differences in team effectiveness. When people trust and like their teammates, they communicate more openly, collaborate more willingly, and work harder to avoid letting each other down

CONFLICT RESOLUTION

My biggest people management mistakes taught me as much as my successes. Times when I misread someone's motivations, made unfair assumptions, or failed to address problems before they escalated. Each mistake was uncomfortable and sometimes damaging to relationships, but they also provided invaluable learning about human nature, communication, and leadership. I learned to apologize when I made mistakes, to adjust my approach based on feedback, and to view relationship problems as learning opportunities rather than just obstacles to overcome.

THE LONG-TERM PERSPECTIVE

Building effective relationships with colleagues wasn't just important for immediate project success. These relationships became the foundation for everything I accomplished later in my career. People who trusted me were more likely to share important information, suggest me for new opportunities, and provide support during challenging periods. They became mentors, collaborators, and advocates throughout my professional development. Investing time and effort in understanding and working effectively with people — even when it seemed less urgent than technical tasks — paid dividends far beyond any individual project or assignment. Managing people effectively wasn't something I mastered quickly or completely. Every new team, every new challenge, every new relationship required me to adapt and learn. But developing these skills became more valuable than any technical expertise I gained, and more important for long-term career success than any individual achievement. The factory taught me that in manufacturing, as in most fields, success ultimately depends on your ability to work effectively with people who are different from you, to build trust and respect across various boundaries, and to bring out the best in others while achieving shared objectives

CHAPTER VIII

NIGHT SHIFT STORIES

You're going on night shift next month," Rajesh sir told me one Thursday afternoon. "It's part of your development. Everyone needs to understand how the factory operates around the clock." I nodded like this was great news, but internally I was panicking. Night shift meant working from 10 PM to 6 AM. It meant my entire schedule getting turned upside down. It meant dealing with different people, different challenges, and a completely different energy on the factory floor. Nothing could have prepared me for how weird and wonderful night shift actually turned out to be

THE ADJUSTMENT PERIOD

You're going on night shift next month," Rajesh sir told me one Thursday afternoon. "It's part of your development. Everyone needs to understand how the factory operates around the clock." I nodded like this was great news, but internally I was panicking. Night shift meant working from 10 PM to 6 AM. It meant my entire schedule getting turned upside down. It meant dealing with different people, different challenges, and a completely different energy on the factory floor. Nothing could have prepared me for how weird and wonderful night shift actually turned out to be

A DIFFERENT WORLD

The factory at night is a completely different place. The daytime chaos and urgency are replaced by a steadier, more focused rhythm. Fewer people, less noise, more space to think and work. The night shift crew is a special breed. These are people who've chosen to work when most of the world sleeps, who've built their lives around this unusual schedule. They're often the most experienced, most self-reliant people in the factory. During the day, there are managers, supervisors, engineers, and support staff everywhere. At night, you have a skeleton crew that has to handle everything themselves. This creates a different kind of teamwork and problem-solving approach. Night shift workers can't wait for the day shift experts to solve problems. They have to figure things out themselves, work with whatever resources are available, and make decisions without layers of approval

CHAPTER VII

THE BROTHERHOOD

There's a camaraderie among night shift workers that's different from any other group I've worked with. Maybe it's because you're all slightly crazy for choosing this lifestyle. Maybe it's because you depend on each other more when fewer people are around. Whatever the reason, night shift people look out for each other in ways that are genuinely touching. Mohan, one of the senior operators, noticed I was struggling with the schedule adjustment. He started bringing extra dinner from home and sharing it with me during our break. "First month is always hard," he said. "You'll figure it out." When someone's car broke down, three people immediately offered rides. When Priya was dealing with a family emergency, the entire shift covered her responsibilities without being asked. This wasn't just professional courtesy — it was genuine care for each other's wellbeing.

DIFFERENT CHALLENGES

Night shift problems are often more urgent because there are fewer people available to help solve them. When a machine breaks down at 2 AM, you can't call in specialists from other departments. You have to work with whoever's on-site. This forces you to become more resourceful, more creative, and more willing to try unconventional solutions. Some of my best learning experiences happened during night shift emergencies when we had to figure out temporary fixes or workarounds under pressure. I remember one night when a control system failed on a critical production line. The normal response would be to call in electrical specialists and wait for repairs. But we were in the middle of an important production run, and delays would affect customer deliveries. Kumar, the night shift electrician, and I spent four hours tracing through circuits, testing components, and eventually identifying a blown fuse that was hidden in an unexpected location. It wasn't glamorous work, but solving that problem at 3 AM felt like winning a championship.

THE QUIET HOURS

The period between 2 AM and 4 AM is unlike anything else in manufacturing. Most of the administrative activity has stopped. Production runs are in steady state. The factory settles into a rhythm that's almost meditative. These were often the times when the best thinking happened. Without constant interruptions and competing demands, you could actually focus on bigger problems, think through complex issues, or plan improvements. I started using these quiet periods for professional development — reading technical articles, researching new approaches, working on project plans. The uninterrupted time was incredibly valuable for deeper thinking. Some of my best ideas came during these late-night reflection periods. Solutions to problems that had been nagging at me for weeks. Insights about process improvements. Clarity about career decisions

CHAPTER VII

THE DAWN SHIFT CHANGE

There's something magical about working through the night and seeing the sun rise as your shift ends. You've been part of keeping the factory running while most people slept. You've solved problems, maintained production, and handed off a smoothly operating facility to the day shift. The shift change at 6 AM had its own ritual. Night shift would brief day shift on any issues, ongoing projects, or things to watch for. There was pride in being able to report that everything was running well, that problems had been handled, that targets had been met. Then you'd walk out into the morning light, feeling the satisfaction of a job well done while most people were just starting their day.

LIFE OUTSIDE THE FACTORY

Night shift affects your entire life, not just your work hours. Social activities have to be scheduled around your sleep schedule. Family time happens at odd hours. Shopping, errands, and appointments all require careful planning. But there are unexpected benefits too. Banks and government offices are less crowded during weekday mornings. Traffic is lighter when you're commuting against the normal flow. You have weekday time for personal activities that are usually crowded with weekend crowds. Some night shift workers become completely nocturnal, structuring their entire lives around the night schedule. Others maintain more conventional weekend schedules and adjust back and forth regularly. I learned to appreciate the flexibility and the different perspective on time that night shift provides.

SKILLS YOU CAN'T LEARN ELSEWHERE

Working night shift teaches you things about self-reliance, problem-solving, and leadership that are hard to develop in normal circumstances. When you're one of only a few people responsible for keeping complex systems running, you develop confidence in your ability to handle whatever comes up. You learn to make decisions without consulting multiple levels of management. You become comfortable with responsibility and accountability. You also learn to work effectively with small teams under pressure. Night shift teams have to be more collaborative and less hierarchical because everyone's contribution is essential. These skills proved valuable throughout my career, even after I moved back to day shift work. The confidence and self-reliance I developed during night shift made me more effective in any challenging situation.

THE CHARACTERS

Night shift attracts interesting people. Some choose it for family reasons — they can be home with kids during the day. Others prefer the different pace and energy. Some are naturally night people who are more alert and productive during late hours. Ramesh had been working nights for ten years because it allowed him to manage his family's farming activities during the day. Sunita preferred nights because she could focus better without the constant interruptions of day shift. Vinod was working nights while completing his engineering degree during the day. Each person had their own story, their own reasons for choosing this lifestyle. Getting to know these stories gave me a much broader perspective on the different ways people structure their lives and careers.

LOOKING BACK

My three months on night shift were among the most valuable of my early career. The experience taught me about self-reliance, teamwork, and problem-solving in ways that normal work situations couldn't. More importantly, it gave me deep respect for the people who keep essential operations running around the clock. Manufacturing doesn't stop for weekends, holidays, or sleep. Someone has to be there, paying attention, solving problems, maintaining the systems that everyone else depends on. When I returned to day shift, I had a completely different appreciation for the complexity and dedication required to run a manufacturing operation continuously. I understood the challenges that night shift workers face and the unique contributions they make. The experience also taught me that stepping outside your comfort zone — even when it's inconvenient or difficult — often provides the most valuable learning opportunities. Night shift wasn't easy, but it made me a better engineer, a better teammate, and a better problem-solver. Years later, when I was in management positions, I always made sure to spend time with night shift workers, to understand their challenges, and to ensure they had the support they needed. That understanding came directly from my own experience working through the night, solving problems in the quiet hours, and being part of the dedicated group of people who keep the factory running while the rest of the world sleeps.

CHAPTER IX

WHEN THE AUDITORS COME CALLING

Audit next week," Rajesh sir announced during our Monday morning meeting. The entire room went quiet. You could feel the collective stress level increase. If you've never worked in manufacturing, you might not understand why a simple audit announcement creates such anxiety. After all, if you're doing your job correctly, what's there to worry about? The answer is: everything.

WHAT AN AUDIT ACTUALLY MEANS

Manufacturing audits aren't like academic exams where you either know the material or you don't. They're comprehensive evaluations of everything — processes, documentation, training records, equipment maintenance, safety procedures, quality controls, environmental compliance. Auditors don't just check whether you're following procedures. They verify that your procedures are correct, that your documentation is complete and current, that your training is adequate, that your results are consistent with your claims. They interview operators to see if they actually understand the procedures they're supposed to follow. They examine equipment to see if it's really maintained according to schedule. They trace through entire processes to identify any gaps or inconsistencies. Most importantly, they assume that if something can go wrong, it probably has gone wrong, and they're going to find evidence of it.

CHAPTER IX

THE AUDIT DAY EXPERIENCE

When auditors actually arrive, the entire atmosphere of the factory changes. Everyone becomes hyperaware of every action, every conversation, every detail that might be observed and evaluated. Auditors are usually polite and professional, but they're also thorough and skeptical. They ask detailed questions about why you do things certain ways. They want to see evidence for every claim you make. They probe for inconsistencies or gaps in your knowledge. I remember following an auditor through our production area during my first audit. She stopped at seemingly random locations and asked specific questions: "How often is this equipment calibrated?" "Who's authorized to perform this operation?" "What happens if this measurement is out of specification?" "Where is this procedure documented?" "When was the last time operators were trained on this process?" Some questions I could answer confidently. Others required me to find documentation or consult with colleagues. A few revealed gaps in my knowledge that were embarrassing but educational.

THE DOCUMENTATION REALITY

One thing audits taught me is the critical importance of documentation in manufacturing. Not just having procedures written down, but keeping them current, making sure they reflect actual practice, and ensuring that everyone understands and follows them. During one audit, an auditor noticed that our written procedure for equipment setup didn't match what operators were actually doing. The operators' method was actually better — more efficient and more reliable. But because it wasn't documented, it looked like we were failing to follow our own procedures. This led to a major effort to review and update all our procedures, ensuring they reflected best practices rather than outdated approaches. It was time-consuming but ultimately made our operations more consistent and effective.

LEARNING FROM AUDIT FINDINGS

Even successful audits usually result in findings — areas where improvements are needed or procedures need clarification. These findings can feel like criticisms, but they're actually opportunities for improvement. I learned to view audit findings as free consulting advice from experts who've seen many different operations. Their observations often identified problems we'd become blind to or suggested approaches we hadn't considered. One auditor pointed out that our quality control process had a potential blind spot — a scenario where defective products could reach customers without being detected. We hadn't experienced this problem, but the risk was real. Implementing the auditor's suggestion prevented what could have been a major customer issue.

CHAPTER IX

THE CONTINUOUS IMPROVEMENT MINDSET

Good audit preparation isn't just about passing the audit — it's about using the audit process to drive continuous improvement. The best managers I worked with used audits as opportunities to systematically review and improve their operations. They'd conduct internal audits using the same standards and approaches that external auditors would use. This helped identify and fix problems before they could affect official audit results. More importantly, they created cultures where people were constantly looking for ways to improve rather than just trying to avoid problems. This proactive approach made audits less stressful and more valuable.

BUILDING AUDIT READINESS

Over time, I learned that the best way to handle audits is to be genuinely audit-ready all the time, not just during preparation periods. This means maintaining documentation consistently, following procedures even when no one's watching, conducting regular self-assessments, and addressing problems immediately rather than letting them accumulate. Organizations that operate this way don't need frantic preparation periods because they're always prepared. Audits become opportunities to showcase good work rather than exercises in crisis management

LONG-TERM BENEFITS

While audits can be stressful, they provide significant long-term benefits. They force organizations to maintain high standards consistently. They identify risks and opportunities that might otherwise be overlooked. They provide benchmarking against industry best practices. Perhaps most importantly, they create accountability. Knowing that your operations will be evaluated by independent experts motivates everyone to maintain high standards and continuous improvement. Organizations that excel at audits usually excel at manufacturing generally. The discipline, attention to detail, and systematic approach required for audit success are the same qualities that drive operational excellence.

PERSONAL GROWTH

Participating in audits taught me valuable skills that extended far beyond manufacturing. How to organize and present information clearly. How to answer challenging questions under pressure. How to identify and address gaps in systems and processes. The experience also taught me to appreciate the value of independent evaluation. Sometimes you're too close to your own work to see problems or opportunities clearly. External perspectives can provide insights that internal reviews miss. Most importantly, audits taught me that accountability isn't something to fear — it's something to embrace. When you're confident in your work and committed to improvement, external evaluation becomes a valuable tool for growth rather than a source of stress. Looking back, every audit I participated in taught me something valuable about manufacturing, about quality, and about myself. They were never easy, but they were always educational. And the lessons I learned from audits made me a better engineer, a better manager, and a better professional overall.

CHAPTER X

MOVING UP THE LADDER

Two years into my manufacturing career, I was starting to feel comfortable. I understood the processes, knew the people, could handle most problems that came up. I was good at my job and enjoying the work. Then Rajesh sir called me into his office for one of those conversations that changes everything. "The company is creating a new position," he said. "Associate Production Manager. It's a step up from engineer — more responsibility, bigger projects, team leadership. I'd like to recommend you for the role." My first reaction was excitement. Recognition! Advancement! More money! My second reaction was panic. Was I ready for this? Could I handle the responsibility? What if I failed?

NEW RESPONSIBILITIES

The promotion came with a significant expansion of responsibilities. Instead of focusing on specific technical problems, I was now responsible for overall production performance in a section that included three production lines, twelve operators, four technicians, and two assistant supervisors. My daily concerns shifted from "How do I solve this problem?" to "How do I ensure problems get solved effectively by other people?" The technical challenges were often easier than the people challenges. Equipment problems had logical causes and systematic solutions. People problems were messier, more complex, and often required solutions that addressed emotions and relationships as much as technical issues.

LEARNING TO DELEGATE

One of my biggest challenges was learning to delegate effectively. As an engineer, I was used to doing technical work myself. As a manager, I had to get work done through other people. This was harder than it sounds. When you delegate a task, you're depending on someone else's understanding, skills, and motivation. You have to provide clear instructions without micromanaging. You have to follow up without being annoying. You have to ensure quality without redoing everything yourself. My first attempts at delegation were disasters. Either I provided too little guidance and people struggled with unclear expectations, or I provided too much guidance and people felt like I didn't trust them. Gradually, I learned that effective delegation requires understanding each person's capabilities, communication style, and motivation level. What works for one person doesn't work for another

CHAPTER X

THE AUTHORITY CHALLENGE

Perhaps the biggest adjustment was learning to exercise authority appropriately. As an engineer, I could influence people through technical expertise and helpful collaboration. As a manager, I sometimes had to make decisions that people didn't like and ensure that those decisions were implemented effectively. This was especially challenging when managing people who were older and more experienced than me. They respected my technical knowledge, but they questioned my judgment on operational decisions. The breakthrough came when I learned to separate personal relationships from professional responsibilities. I could be friendly and respectful with everyone while still maintaining clear expectations and accountability. It helped to explain my reasoning for decisions, especially when they affected people's work routines. People might not always agree with my decisions, but they respected them more when they understood the logic behind them

STRATEGIC THINKING

Manager-level decisions required longer-term thinking than I was used to. Instead of focusing on immediate problems, I had to anticipate future challenges and opportunities. This meant understanding business trends that could affect our operations. Technology developments that could improve our processes. Competitive pressures that could change our requirements. Regulatory changes that could affect our procedures. I started reading industry publications, attending conferences, and networking with colleagues at other companies. The perspective I gained from these activities helped me make better decisions and identify opportunities for improvement.

TEAM DEVELOPMENT

One of the most rewarding aspects of the management role was helping other people develop their capabilities. Instead of just focusing on my own learning and advancement, I could contribute to other people's career growth. This meant identifying each person's strengths and development needs. Providing opportunities for them to learn new skills. Giving them challenging assignments that stretched their capabilities. Offering feedback and coaching to help them improve. Some people thrived with additional responsibility and learning opportunities. Others preferred stable, predictable work and weren't interested in advancement. Learning to work with these different motivations and career goals required understanding each person as an individual

CHAPTER X

WORK-LIFE BALANCE CHALLENGES

The increased responsibility also brought increased time demands. Problems that arose during off-hours often required my attention. Planning and coordination activities extended beyond normal working hours. The mental load of responsibility was difficult to set aside at the end of the day. Learning to manage these demands while maintaining personal health and relationships became a new challenge. I had to develop better time management skills, learn to prioritize more effectively, and find ways to disconnect from work when necessary. This balance was an ongoing challenge throughout my management career. The people who succeeded long-term were those who found sustainable approaches to handling responsibility without sacrificing everything else in their lives.

MEASURING SUCCESS

Success as a manager was measured differently than success as an engineer. Instead of individual technical achievements, success was measured by team performance, operational results, and development of people. This shift in focus required learning to find satisfaction in other people's achievements rather than just my own accomplishments. When team members solved problems effectively, improved their skills, or achieved their career goals, their success became my success. It also meant accepting responsibility for failures, even when they weren't directly caused by my decisions. When the team didn't meet objectives, I had to understand what went wrong and how to prevent similar problems in the future.

LONG-TERM IMPACT

The management role fundamentally changed my perspective on manufacturing and my career. Instead of focusing primarily on technical challenges, I began to understand the business context that drives all manufacturing decisions. I learned to think systematically about how different factors — technology, people, processes, costs, customer requirements — interact to determine overall performance. This systems thinking became valuable for every subsequent role in my career. Most importantly, I learned that leadership is a skill that can be developed through practice, feedback, and conscious effort. Nobody is born knowing how to manage people effectively, but everyone can learn if they're willing to put in the effort and learn from their mistakes. The transition to management wasn't easy, and I made plenty of mistakes along the way. But it opened up opportunities and responsibilities that made my career more interesting, more challenging, and ultimately more rewarding than anything I could have achieved as an individual contributor

CHAPTER XI

LOOKING FORWARD

Five years into my manufacturing career, I've learned enough to know how much I still don't know. Every day brings new challenges, new learning opportunities, and new perspectives on what it means to work in this industry. But I've also learned enough to have opinions about where manufacturing is heading, what opportunities exist for young professionals, and what it takes to build a successful career in this field.

THE CHANGING FACE OF MANUFACTURING

Indian manufacturing today is nothing like what it was even a decade ago. The factories I visit now are implementing technologies that were science fiction when I started my career. Automated systems that adjust processes in real-time based on quality measurements. Predictive maintenance that identifies potential equipment failures weeks before they occur. Digital systems that track every component from raw material to finished product. But the most important changes aren't just technological — they're cultural. Manufacturing companies are investing heavily in employee development, workplace safety, and environmental sustainability. The old stereotypes about manufacturing work are becoming increasingly outdated. The best companies now offer career development programs, tuition assistance, and advancement opportunities that rival any industry. They're creating work environments that attract talented people and give them reasons to stay and grow.

CHAPTER XI

OPPORTUNITIES FOR YOUTH

For young engineers entering manufacturing today, the opportunities are extraordinary. This industry is hungry for people who combine technical knowledge with fresh perspectives, who can bridge the gap between traditional manufacturing wisdom and modern technological capabilities. The aging workforce in many factories means that advancement opportunities are opening up faster than in most other industries. Companies are actively looking for young professionals who can take on leadership roles and drive innovation. But success requires more than just technical education. The most successful young professionals I've worked with are those who've developed strong communication skills, cultural awareness, and practical problem-solving abilities. They understand that manufacturing success depends as much on working effectively with people as it does on understanding machines and processes.

THE SKILLS THAT MATTER

Based on my experience and observations, certain skills are becoming increasingly important for manufacturing professionals:

Systems thinking — Understanding how different parts of complex operations interact and affect each other.

Continuous learning — Technology and processes evolve constantly, requiring ongoing skill development.

Cultural adaptability — Manufacturing operations are increasingly global, requiring ability to work effectively across different cultures and communication styles.

Digital literacy — Even traditional manufacturing roles now require comfort with digital tools and data analysis.

Leadership development — Career advancement in manufacturing increasingly requires ability to lead teams and manage operations.

But the most important skill is something that can't be taught in textbooks: the ability to remain calm and effective under pressure while maintaining genuine concern for the people you work with.

CHAPTER XI

PERSONAL GOALS AND ASPIRATIONS

Looking ahead, my own goals have evolved significantly from when I started. Instead of just focusing on technical advancement, I'm thinking about broader impact and contribution. I want to be part of the generation that transforms manufacturing from a necessary but unglamorous industry into a respected and attractive career choice for India's best young talent. I want to help develop workplace cultures that combine operational excellence with genuine concern for employee development and wellbeing. I want to contribute to manufacturing operations that are not just profitable, but genuinely sustainable and beneficial for the communities they serve. On a personal level, I want to continue developing my leadership capabilities, not just for career advancement, but to become someone who can bring out the best in other people and help them achieve their own goals

THE SUSTAINABILITY CHALLENGE

Manufacturing faces enormous challenges related to environmental sustainability, resource efficiency, and social responsibility. These challenges create opportunities for innovative solutions and new approaches to traditional problems. The next generation of manufacturing leaders will need to balance economic performance with environmental stewardship. This requires technical innovation, but also new ways of thinking about success and value creation. I believe manufacturing can be part of the solution to environmental challenges rather than just part of the problem. But this requires conscious effort from everyone in the industry to prioritize long-term sustainability over short-term convenience.

WORK-LIFE INTEGRATION

One area where I'm still learning is how to integrate career ambitions with personal life goals. Manufacturing careers often involve demanding schedules, high-pressure environments, and significant responsibility. Finding sustainable approaches to this challenge is crucial for long-term success and personal satisfaction. The people I most admire in this industry are those who've found ways to excel professionally while maintaining strong relationships and personal interests outside of work

PERSONAL GOALS AND ASPIRATIONS

This balance looks different for different people, but it requires conscious effort and regular adjustment as circumstances change.

Advice for Newcomers

For anyone considering a manufacturing career, here's what I would recommend:

Start with realistic expectations.

Manufacturing work is demanding, and advancement requires both technical competence and people skills. But the opportunities for meaningful contribution and career growth are genuine.

Focus on learning from everyone.

Some of the most valuable insights come from experienced operators and technicians who understand practical aspects of manufacturing that aren't covered in textbooks.

Develop both technical and interpersonal skills.

Success requires competence in both areas, and neither alone is sufficient for long-term advancement.

Embrace challenges.

The most valuable learning experiences often come from situations that push you outside your comfort zone.

Take care of yourself.

Manufacturing careers can be demanding, so developing sustainable approaches to managing stress and maintaining perspective is crucial.

Build genuine relationships.

Success in manufacturing depends heavily on ability to work effectively with diverse groups of people under challenging circumstances.

THE BIGGER PICTURE

Manufacturing isn't just about making products — it's about creating the foundation for economic development, technological innovation, and social progress. When manufacturing thrives, it creates employment opportunities, drives technological advancement, and contributes to national economic strength. When it struggles, the effects ripple through entire communities and regions. Being part of this industry means contributing to something larger than individual career success. It means being part of the economic engine that enables everything else society depends on. This perspective makes the daily challenges and frustrations worthwhile. Even difficult days contribute to something meaningful and important.

CHAPTER XI

FINAL THOUGHTS

My manufacturing career has been more challenging and more rewarding than anything I could have anticipated when I started. It's taught me about technology, about business, about leadership, and about myself. Most importantly, it's connected me with an industry and a community of people who are building the future through practical, meaningful work. For young professionals considering manufacturing careers, I can't promise it will be easy. But I can promise it will be real, it will be important, and it will provide opportunities for growth and contribution that are difficult to find elsewhere. The manufacturing industry needs talented, motivated people who are willing to learn, adapt, and contribute. For those who are ready for the challenge, the opportunities are extraordinary. The future of Indian manufacturing depends on attracting and developing the next generation of leaders. I'm proud to be part of that effort, and excited about what we can accomplish together.

CONCLUSION

When I first walked onto that factory floor seven years ago, I thought manufacturing was about machines, processes, and technical problems. I had no idea it was really about people, relationships, and constant learning. The journey from nervous new engineer to confident manager has taught me lessons I never could have learned anywhere else. About leadership under pressure. About working with people who are different from you. About finding solutions when the textbook answers don't work. About taking responsibility for results that affect real people and real businesses. More than anything, it's taught me that manufacturing is fundamentally about service — serving customers who depend on your products, serving colleagues who count on your contribution, serving communities that benefit from the economic opportunities that manufacturing creates. This book is my attempt to share what I've learned, especially with young people who might be considering manufacturing careers. It's not a complete guide — everyone's experience is different — but it's an honest account of what this journey has been like for me. Manufacturing isn't glamorous work. It won't make you social media famous or get you invited to startup conferences. But it will teach you things about problem-solving, leadership, and resilience that serve you well in any career. And it will connect you with an industry that's essential for economic development and technological progress. For young engineers, technicians, and managers entering manufacturing: the challenges are real, but so are the opportunities. This industry needs talented people who are willing to learn, adapt, and contribute. If you're ready for the challenge, manufacturing can provide a career that's meaningful, rewarding, and constantly evolving. To my colleagues in manufacturing: thank you for the lessons, the support, and the inspiration. This industry is stronger because of people who take pride in their work and care about each other's success. And to everyone who's curious about what happens inside those factory buildings on the outskirts of every Indian city: this is our story. We're the people who make the things that make everything else possible. We're proud of that responsibility, and we're working every day to do it better. The future of Indian manufacturing is bright, and it's being built by young professionals who combine technical expertise with genuine concern for people and communities. I'm honored to be part of that effort. Here's to more hard hats, more hustle, and more young people discovering that manufacturing offers something special: the chance to build the future with your own hands.

ACKNOWLEDGMENTS

This book wouldn't exist without the countless colleagues, mentors, and friends who shared their knowledge, patience, and support throughout my manufacturing journey.

To the operators, technicians, and supervisors who taught me that practical wisdom often matters more than theoretical knowledge.

To the managers and leaders who gave me opportunities to learn, grow, and take on responsibilities that stretched my capabilities.

To my family and friends who supported me through the challenging early years and celebrated the successes along the way.

And to the manufacturing industry itself, for providing challenges that forced me to grow and opportunities that exceeded my expectations.

Thank you all for making this journey possible and this book necessary.

"Rautela captures both the challenges and the satisfaction of manufacturing work. A must-read for anyone considering this path"

Also by the Author
MobCast Podcast - Career Stories from Indian Engineers